W9-AYZ-879

First Facts®

The Solar System

Space Junk

by Steve Kortenkamp

Consultant:
James Gerard
Aerospace Education Specialist, NASA
Kennedy Space Center, Florida

Capstone
press®

Mankato, Minnesota

First Facts is published by Capstone Press,
151 Good Counsel Drive, P.O. Box 669, Mankato, Minnesota 56002.
www.capstonepress.com

Library of Congress Cataloging-in-Publication Data
Kortenkamp, Steve.
    Space junk / by Steve Kortenkamp.
    p. cm. — (First facts. The solar system)
    Summary: "Describes the types of debris orbiting Earth and discusses the hazards space junk
presents to spacecraft and astronauts" — Provided by publisher.
    Includes bibliographical references and index.
    ISBN-13: 978-1-4296-1258-6 (hardcover)
    ISBN-10: 1-4296-1258-4 (hardcover)
    1. Space debris — Juvenile literature. I. Title. II. Series.
TL1499.K67 2008
363.12'41 — dc22   2007023027

Editorial Credits
Lori Shores and Christopher L. Harbo, editors; Juliette Peters, set designer;
    Kim Brown, book designer and illustrator; Linda Clavel, photo researcher

Photo Credits
Capstone Press/Kim Brown, cover; Kim Brown and Scott Thoms, 10–11
Corbis/Bettmann, 6; Reuters, 18
NASA, 1, 5, 7, 9, 12, 13, 14, 19, 20
Photodisc, back cover
U.S. Air Force, 16–17
Wikipedia, public-domain image, 21

1 2 3 4 5 6 13 12 11 10 09 08

Table of Contents

What Is Space Junk?

Wherever people go, they usually make a lot of garbage. Ever since people have been going to space, garbage has been gathering there too. When this trash **orbits** Earth, it's called space junk. Space junk includes everything from used rockets to broken spacecraft to tools lost by astronauts.

Fun Fact!

In 1965, astronaut Edward White lost a spare glove during the first American space walk.

The First Space Junk

Junk has littered space since Russia launched the first **satellite**, *Sputnik*, in 1957. It worked for a few days. Then it became the first piece of space junk.

In 1958, the United States launched the *Explorer 1* satellite. It lasted only four months. After that, it too was a piece of space junk.

Are Astronauts Litterbugs?

Astronauts sometimes lose things on **space walks**, but it isn't garbage they are tossing. They've lost nuts, bolts, and even cameras. These things floated away into space.

In 2006, astronauts pushed an empty space suit into space as an experiment. The suit sent out a radio message for a short time. Then it became space junk.

! Fun Fact!
People on Earth could listen to the space suit's message on radios. The message was "This is SuitSat."

SuitSat

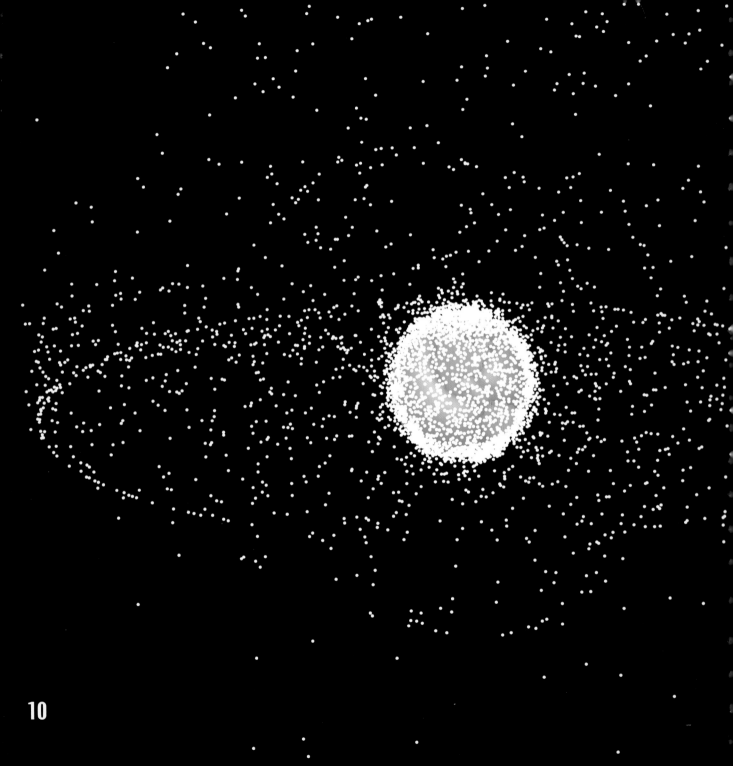

Earth's Ring of Junk

Jupiter, Saturn, Uranus, and Neptune all have rings around them. But these planets aren't the only ones with rings. Our planet has one too! But Earth's ring is made up of millions of pieces of space junk, not gasses and rocks.

! Fun Fact!
The outer edge of Earth's ring of space junk is more than 23,000 miles (37,015 kilometers) from the planet.

Space Junk Is Dangerous

Space junk is dangerous because it travels 30 times faster than a bullet. In 2006, a small piece of space junk punched a hole in the space shuttle *Atlantis*.

Space junk can also harm astronauts on space walks. Astronauts must wear protective space suits. These suits are made from the material used in bulletproof vests.

Tracking Space Junk

Scientists use **telescopes** and **radar** to track space junk. Radar can find and measure the speed of tiny pieces of space junk.

Scientists warn astronauts when space junk might run into the *International Space Station*. Astronauts use rockets to move the station out of the way.

! Fun Fact!
Radar can detect pieces of space junk as small as an ant!

Making More Space Junk

Spacecraft and satellites often break apart when they hit space junk. Scientists must then track hundreds of tiny, new pieces of junk. Someday, too much junk could make the space around Earth unsafe for satellites, spacecraft, and astronauts.

Fun Fact!
In 2007, a Chinese missile blew up an old satellite. The explosion created more than 1 million pieces of space junk.

Cleaning Up Space Junk

Some space junk is cleaned up naturally by Earth's **atmosphere**. The junk burns up as it falls through the atmosphere. In 2001, an old space station named *Mir* burned up as it fell to Earth.

Sometimes junk makes it through the atmosphere. Most junk falls into the ocean, but some junk hits land. Then people need to clean it up.

Rocket fuel tank that fell to Earth

Amazing but True!

Not all space junk orbits Earth. Some junk has been left on the Moon, Venus, and Mars. Space junk has even left our solar system. The *Pioneer 11* space probe was launched in 1973. Now it is drifting through the galaxy. It will pass by a distant star in about 3 million years.

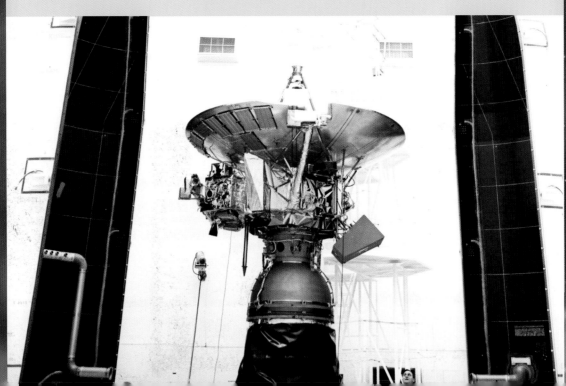

Think Big!

Earth's atmosphere cleans up some space junk. But many pieces of junk orbit far from the atmosphere. Scientists are studying ways to use **lasers** to clean up space junk. Lasers may be able to knock pieces of space junk into the atmosphere to burn up. Can you think of other ways to clean up space junk?

Glossary

atmosphere (AT-muh-sfeehr) — the mixture of gases that surrounds some planets and moons

laser (LAY-zur) — a thin, high-energy beam of light

orbit (OR-bit) — to circle another object in space

radar (RAY-dar) — a device that uses radio waves to locate distant objects

satellite (SAT-uh-lite) — a spacecraft that circles Earth; satellites take pictures and send messages to Earth.

space walk (SPAYSS WAWK) — a period of time during which an astronaut leaves the spacecraft to move around in space

telescope (TEL-uh-skope) — a tool that makes faraway objects look larger and closer

Read More

Asimov, Isaac, and Richard Hantula. *Space Junk.* Isaac Asimov's 21st Century Library of the Universe. Milwaukee: Gareth Stevens, 2006.

Johnson, Rebecca L. *Satellites.* Cool Science. Minneapolis: Lerner, 2006.

Rau, Dana Meachen. *The International Space Station.* Our Solar System. Minneapolis: Compass Point Books, 2005.

Internet Sites

FactHound offers a safe, fun way to find Internet sites related to this book. All of the sites on FactHound have been researched by our staff.

Here's how:
1. Visit *www.facthound.com*
2. Choose your grade level.
3. Type in this book ID **1429612584** for age-appropriate sites. You may also browse subjects by clicking on letters, or by clicking on pictures and words.
4. Click on the **Fetch It** button.

Facthound will fetch the best sites for you!

Index